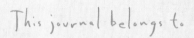

This journal belongs to

....

AUDUBON
American Robin

For I know the plans... Butterfly Journal

© 2011 Ellie Claire Gift & Paper Corp.

www.ellieclaire.com

Compiled by Barbara Farmer
Designed by Lisa and Jeff Franke

ISBN 978-1-60936-235-5

For I know
the PLANS I have
for YOU.

JEREMIAH 29:11

Ellie
Claire
gift & paper expressions

...inspired by life

What we feel, think, and do this moment influences both our present and the future in ways we may never know. Begin. Start right where you are. Consider your possibilities and find inspiration...to add more meaning and zest to your life.

Alexandra Stoddard

*N*o eye has seen, no ear has heard, and no mind has imagined
what God has prepared for those who love Him.

1 Corinthians 2:9 NLT

Graduation is only a concept. In real life every day you graduate.
Graduation is a process that goes on until the last day of your life.
If you can grasp that, you'll make a difference.

Arie Pencovici

....

....

....

....

....

....

....

....

....

....

....

....

....

....

....

....

....

*G*et the word out. Teach all these things.... Immerse yourself in them.
The people will all see you mature right before their eyes!
Keep a firm grasp on both your character and your teaching.

1 Timothy 4:11, 15-16 THE MESSAGE

The future belongs to those who believe in the beauty of their dreams.

Eleanor Roosevelt

And let the beauty of the Lord our God be upon us, and establish the work of our hands for us; yes, establish the work of our hands.

Psalm 90:17 NKJV

A dream becomes a goal when action is taken toward its achievement.

Bo Bennett

*D*ear brothers and sisters, I have not achieved it, but I focus on this one thing: Forgetting the past and looking forward to what lies ahead, I press on to reach the end of the race and receive the heavenly prize for which God, through Christ Jesus, is calling us.

Philippians 3:13-14 NLT

*S*ociety needs people who...know how to be compassionate and honest.... Society needs all kinds of skills that are not just cognitive; they're emotional, they're affectional. You can't run the society on data and computers alone.

Alvin Toffler

....

....

....

....

....

....

....

....

....

....

....

....

....

....

....

....

....

....

....

What happens when we live God's way? He brings gifts into our lives...
things like affection for others, exuberance about life..., a sense of compassion in
the heart, and a conviction that a basic holiness permeates things and people.

Galatians 5:22-23 THE MESSAGE

The best way to lead is by a good example.

Among you it will be different. Whoever wants to be
a leader among you must be your servant.

Mark 10:43 NLT

You are educated. Your certification is in your degree. You may think of it as the ticket to the good life. Let me ask you to think of an alternative. Think of it as your ticket to change the world.

Tom Brokaw

_M_ake sure you don't take things for granted and go slack in working for the common good; share what you have with others. God takes particular pleasure in acts of worship...that take place in kitchen and workplace and on the streets.

Hebrews 13:16 THE MESSAGE

Many an opportunity is lost because one is out looking for four-leaf clovers.

*L*et us not grow weary while doing good, for in due season we shall reap if we do not lose heart. Therefore, as we have opportunity, let us do good to all.

Galatians 6:9-10 NKJV

Perseverance is a great element of success. If you only knock long enough and loud enough at the gate, you are sure to wake up somebody.

Henry Wadsworth Longfellow

Ask and it will be given to you; seek and you will find; knock and the door
will be opened to you. For everyone who asks receives; he who seeks finds;
and to him who knocks, the door will be opened.

Matthew 7:7-8 NIV

*G*od has designs on our future...and He has designed us for the future.
He has given us something to do in the future that no one else can do.

Ruth Senter

have it all planned out—plans to take care of you, not abandon you,
plans to give you the future you hope for.

Jeremiah 29:11 THE MESSAGE

*S*hoot for the moon. Even if you miss, you'll land among the stars.

Les Brown

Every good action and every perfect gift is from God. These good
gifts come down from the Creator of the sun, moon, and stars,
who does not change like their shifting shadows.

James 1:17 NCV

*L*eaders learn by leading, and they learn best by leading in the face of obstacles. As weather shapes mountains, problems shape leaders.

Warren G. Bennis

*C*onsider it pure joy...whenever you face trials of many kinds, because you know that the testing of your faith develops perseverance. Perseverance must finish its work so that you may be mature and complete, not lacking anything.

James 1:2-4 NIV

In the business world, everyone is paid in two coins: cash and experience.
Take the experience first; the cash will come later.

Harold Geneen

*W*ealth from get-rich-quick schemes quickly disappears;
wealth from hard work grows over time.

Proverbs 13:11 NLT

*G*o confidently in the direction of your dreams.
Live the life you have imagined.

Henry David Thoreau

have come that they may have life, and that they
may have it more abundantly.

John 10:10 NKJV

You have brains in your head. You have feet in your shoes.
You can steer yourself in any direction you choose.
You're on your own. And you know what you know.
You are the one who'll decide where to go.

Dr. Seuss

The Lord directs the steps of the godly. He delights in every detail of their lives.
Though they stumble, they will never fall, for the Lord holds them by the hand.

Psalm 37:23-24 NLT

Today is unique! It has never occurred before and it will never be repeated. At midnight it will end, quietly, suddenly, totally. Forever. But the hours between now and then are opportunities with eternal possibilities.

Charles R. Swindoll

This is the day the Lord has made;
we will rejoice and be glad in it.

Psalm 118:24 NKJV

The future lies before you like a field of driven snow,
Be careful how you tread it, for every step will show.

The highway of the upright avoids evil;
he who guards his way guards his life.

Proverbs 16:17 NIV

Every failure, obstacle or hardship is an opportunity in disguise.
Success in many cases is failure turned inside out.

Mary Kay Ash

My child, do not forget my teaching, but keep my commands in mind.
Then you will live a long time, and your life will be successful.

Proverbs 3:1-2 NCV

You are not here merely to make a living. You are here in order to enable the world to live more amply, with greater vision, with a finer spirit of hope and achievement. You are here to enrich the world, and you impoverish yourself if you forget the errand.

Woodrow Wilson

May the God of hope fill you with all joy and peace as you trust in Him,
so that you may overflow with hope by the power of the Holy Spirit.

Romans 15:13 NIV

The leadership instinct you are born with is the backbone.
You develop the funny bone and the wishbone that go with it.

Elaine Agather

*H*e will yet fill your mouth with laughter
and your lips with shouts of joy.

Job 12:8 NIV

*D*on't judge each day by the harvest you reap but by the seeds that you plant.

Robert Louis Stevenson

Plant your seed in the morning and keep busy all afternoon, for you don't know if profit will come from one activity or another—or maybe both.

Ecclesiastes 11:6 NLT

All who have accomplished great things have had a great aim, have fixed their gaze on a goal which was high, one which sometimes seemed impossible.

Orison Swett Marden

....
....
....
....
....
....
....
....
....
....
....
....
....
....
....
....
....
....

'm not saying that I have this all together, that I have it made. But I am well on my way, reaching out for Christ, who has so wondrously reached out for me.

Philippians 3:12 THE MESSAGE

The larger the island of knowledge, the longer the shoreline of wonder.

Ralph W. Sockman

will praise You, for I am fearfully and wonderfully made;
marvelous are Your works, and that my soul knows very well.

Psalm 139:14 NKJV

*I*f leaders are filled with high ambition and if they pursue their aims with audacity and strength of will, they will reach them in spite of all obstacles.

Carl von Clausewitz

*P*ursue a righteous life—a life of wonder, faith, love, steadiness, courtesy.
Run hard and fast in the faith. Seize the eternal life, the life you were called to,
the life you so fervently embraced in the presence of so many witnesses.

1 Timothy 6:11-12 THE MESSAGE

No matter what your age or your situation, your dreams are achievable.
Whether you're five or 105, you have a lifetime ahead of you!

Oh, how sweet the light of day, and how wonderful to live in the sunshine!
Even if you live a long time, don't take a single day for granted.
Take delight in each light-filled hour.

Ecclesiastes 11:7-8 THE MESSAGE

Those who build the future are those who know that greater things are yet to come, and that they themselves will help bring them about.

Melvin J. Evans

*L*ook at those who are honest and good, for a wonderful
future awaits those who love peace.

Psalm 37:37 NLT

*G*et over the idea that only children should spend their time in study. Be a student so long as you still have something to learn, and this will mean all your life.

Henry L. Doherty

'm asking God for one thing, only one thing: To live with Him in His house my whole life long. I'll contemplate His beauty; I'll study at His feet.

Psalm 27:4 THE MESSAGE

*Don't be afraid to take a big step if one is indicated;
you can't cross a chasm in two small jumps.*

David Lloyd George

*D*aughter, you took a risk trusting Me, and now you're healed and whole.
Live well, live blessed!

Luke 8:48 THE MESSAGE

*K*eep in mind that neither success nor failure is ever final.

Roger Babson

May He grant you according to your heart's desire,
And fulfill all your purpose.

Psalm 20:4 NKJV

Common sense is the measure of the possible; it is composed of experience and prevision; it is calculation applied to life.

Henri Frédéric Amiel

For the Lord grants wisdom! From His mouth come knowledge and understanding. He grants a treasure of common sense to the honest. He is a shield to those who walk with integrity.

Proverbs 2:6–7 NLT

*L*ife is my college. May I graduate well, and earn some honors!

Louisa May Alcott

Always pursue what is good both for yourselves and for all. Rejoice always, pray without ceasing, in everything give thanks.... Test all things; hold fast what is good.

1 Thessalonians 5:15-18, 21 NKJV

You can't live a perfect day without doing something for someone who will never be able to repay you.

John Wooden

When you give a dinner or a supper, do not ask...your relatives, nor rich neighbors, lest they also invite you back, and you be repaid. But...invite the poor, the maimed, the lame, the blind. And you will be blessed.

Luke 14:12-14 NKJV

Goals provide the energy source that powers our lives. One of the best ways we can get the most from the energy we have is to focus it. That is what goals can do for us: concentrate our energy.

Denis Waitley

*K*eep your eyes focused on what is right, and look
straight ahead to what is good.

Proverbs 4:25 NCV

Most of the important things in the world have been accomplished by people who have kept on trying when there seemed to be no hope at all.

Dale Carnegie

We also rejoice in our sufferings, because we know that suffering produces perseverance; perseverance, character; and character, hope. And hope does not disappoint us, because God has poured out His love into our hearts.

Romans 5:3-5 NIV

It's what you learn after you know it all that counts.

Harry S. Truman

A wise man will hear and increase learning, and a man
of understanding will attain wise counsel.

Proverbs 1:5 NKJV

*N*othing is as real as a dream. The world can change around you, but your dream will not. Responsibilities need not erase it. Duties need not obscure it. Because the dream is within you, no one can take it away.

Tom Clancy

··

··

··

··

··

··

··

··

··

··

··

··

··

··

*T*here is surely a future hope for you,
and your hope will not be cut off.

Proverbs 23:18 NIV

*T*he important thing really is not the deed well done or the medal that you possess, but the dedication and dreams out of which they grow.

Robert H. Benson

*S*teep your life in God-reality, God-initiative, God-provisions. Don't worry about missing out. You'll find all your everyday human concerns will be met.

Matthew 6:33 THE MESSAGE

Things turn out best for the people who make the best
out of the way things turn out.

Art Linkletter

*Y*ou were taught, with regard to your former way of life, to put off your old self...; to be made new in the attitude of your minds.

Ephesians 4:22-23 NIV

$\mathscr{Y}$ou learn something every day if you pay attention.

Ray LeBlond

Pay close attention, friend, to what your father tells you; never forget what you learned at your mother's knee. Wear their counsel like flowers in your hair, like rings on your fingers.

Proverbs 1:8-9 THE MESSAGE

*T*here's no thrill in easy sailing when the skies are clear and blue,
There's no joy in merely doing things which anyone can do.
But there is some satisfaction that is mighty sweet to take,
when you reach a destination that you thought you'd never make.

Wise words bring many benefits, and hard work brings rewards.

Proverbs 12:14 NLT

You can't experience success beyond your wildest dreams until you dare to dream something wild!

Scott Sorrell

*G*od can do anything, you know—far more than you could ever
imagine or guess or request in your wildest dreams!

Ephesians 3:20 THE MESSAGE

Vision looks inwards and becomes duty. Vision looks outwards and becomes aspiration. Vision looks upwards and becomes faith.

Stephen Samuel Wise

Be joyful in hope, patient in affliction, faithful in prayer.

Romans 12:12 NIV

The first responsibility of a leader is to define reality. The last is to say thank you. In between, the leader is a servant.

Max De Pree

*W*hoever wants to be a leader among you must be your servant.

Matthew 20:26 NLT

Action springs not from thought, but from a readiness for responsibility.

Dietrich Bonhoeffer

Each person should judge his own actions and not compare himself with others. Then he can be proud for what he himself has done. Each person must be responsible for himself.

Galatians 6:4-5 NCV

The purpose of learning is growth, and our minds, unlike our bodies, can continue growing as we continue to live.

Mortimer Adler

The mind of a person with understanding gets knowledge;
the wise person listens to learn more.

Proverbs 18:15 NCV

This is your moment! Throw off the lines. Leave behind the safe harbor. Catch the wind and sail into the open waters. Seek adventure. Go after your dreams. Discover your life.

*D*ear friend, listen well to my words.... Those who discover these words live, really live; body and soul.... Keep vigilant watch over your heart; *that's* where life starts.

Proverbs 4:20-23 THE MESSAGE

*M*ake the most of yourself, for that is all there is of you.

Ralph Waldo Emerson

*B*e wise in the way you act...; make the most of every opportunity.
Let your conversation be always full of grace, seasoned with salt,
so that you may know how to answer everyone.

Colossians 4:5-6 NIV

When you come to the end of all the light you know, and it's time to step into the darkness of the unknown, faith is knowing that one of two things shall happen: Either you will be given something solid to stand on or you will be taught to fly.

Edward Teller

For we walk by faith, not by sight.

2 Corinthians 5:7 NKJV

*T*hose who will use their skill and constructive imagination to see how much they can give for a dollar, instead of how little they can give for a dollar, are bound to succeed.

Henry Ford

This service you do not only helps the needs of God's people, it also brings many more thanks to God. It is a proof of your faith. Many people will praise God because you obey the Good News...and because you freely share with them and with all others.

2 Corinthians 9:12-13 NCV

I am defeated, and know it, if I meet any human being from whom I find myself unable to learn anything.

George Herbert Palmer

....

....

....

....

....

....

....

....

....

....

....

....

....

....

....

....

Teach the wise, and they will become even wiser; teach good people,
and they will learn even more.

Proverbs 9:9 NCV

It is not in the pursuit of happiness that we find fulfillment,
it is in the happiness of pursuit.

Denis Waitley

*H*e who pursues righteousness and love finds life, prosperity and honor.

Proverbs 21:21 NIV

No matter how some may think themselves accomplished, when they set out to learn a new language, science, or the bicycle, they have entered a new realm as truly as if they were a child newly born into the world.

Frances Willard

May He give you the power to accomplish all the good
things your faith prompts you to do.

2 Thessalonians 1:11 NLT

The difference between perseverance and obstinacy is that one often comes from a strong will, and the other from a strong won't.

Henry Ward Beecher

God blesses those who patiently endure testing and temptation. Afterward they will receive the crown of life that God has promised to those who love him.

James 1:12 NLT

Hope, in this deep and powerful sense, is not the same as joy that things are going well, or willingness to invest in enterprises that are obviously heading for success, but rather an ability to work for something because it is good.

Václav Havel

will praise You forever for what You have done; in Your name I will hope, for Your name is good. I will praise You in the presence of Your saints.

Psalm 52:9 NIV

The golden opportunity you are seeking is in yourself. It is not in your environment; it is not in luck or chance, or the help of others; it is in yourself alone.

Orison Swett Marden

So, friends, confirm God's invitation to you, His choice of you. Don't put it off; do it now. Do this, and you'll have your life on a firm footing.

2 Peter 1:10-11 THE MESSAGE

The best helping hand that you will ever receive is
the one at the end of your own arm.

Fred Dehner

*R*emind the people...to be ready to do whatever is good,...to be peaceable
and considerate, and to show true humility toward all men.

Titus 3:1-2 NIV

*W*henever it is possible, choose some occupation which you should do even if you did not need the money.

William Lyon Phelps

*D*o your work with enthusiasm. Work as if you were serving the Lord, not as if you were serving only men and women. Remember that the Lord will give a reward to everyone...for doing good.

Ephesians 6:7-8 NCV

A span of life is nothing. But the man or woman who lives that span, they are something. They can fill that tiny span with meaning, so its quality is immeasurable, though its quantity may be insignificant.

Chaim Potok

And I pray that you...will have the power to understand the greatness of Christ's love—how wide and how long and how high and how deep that love is.... Then you can be filled with the fullness of God.

Ephesians 3:18-19 NCV

*I*n simplest terms, leaders are those who know where they want to go, and get up, and go.

John Erskine

*T*herefore, since we are surrounded by such a huge crowd of witnesses
to the life of faith, let us strip off every weight that slows us down....
And let us run with endurance the race God has set before us.

Hebrews 12:1 NLT

The greatest pollution problem we face today is negativity.
Eliminate the negative attitude and believe you can do anything.
Replace "if I can, I hope, maybe" with "I can, I will, I must."

Mary Kay Ash

....

....

....

....

....

....

....

....

....

....

....

....

....

....

....

....

....

....

....

*B*e kindly affectionate to one another...; not lagging in diligence, fervent in spirit,
serving the Lord; rejoicing in hope, patient in tribulation, continuing steadfastly
in prayer; distributing to the needs of the saints, given to hospitality.

Romans 12:10-13 NKJV

Anyone who stops learning is old, whether at twenty or eighty.

Henry Ford

*C*ease listening to instruction...and you will
stray from the words of knowledge.

Proverbs 17:27 NKJV

*L*ife is not easy for any of us. But what of that? We must have perseverance and above all confidence in ourselves. We must believe that we are gifted for something and that this thing must be attained.

Marie Curie

*E*ach of you has received a gift to use to serve others.
Be good servants of God's various gifts of grace.

1 Peter 4:10 NCV

Wise are those who learn that the bottom line doesn't
always have to be their top priority.

William A. Ward

A good name is to be chosen rather than great riches,
Loving favor rather than silver and gold.

Proverbs 22:1 NKJV

Don't ever let yourself get so busy that you miss those little but important extras in life—the beauty of a day...the smile of a friend.... For it is often life's smallest pleasures and gentlest joys that make the biggest and most lasting difference.

It is not fancy hair, gold jewelry, or fine clothes that should make you beautiful.
No, your beauty should come from within you—the beauty of a gentle and quiet
spirit that will never be destroyed and is very precious to God.

1 Peter 3:3-4 NCV

There are no shortcuts to any place worth going.

Beverly Sills

For what profit is it to a man if he gains the
whole world, and loses his own soul?

Matthew 16:26 NKJV

*S*omehow I can't believe that there are any heights that can't be scaled by a person who knows the secrets of making dreams come true. This special secret...can be summarized in four Cs. They are curiosity, confidence, courage, and constancy.

Walt Disney

*H*oney from the honeycomb tastes sweet. In the same way, wisdom is pleasing to you. If you find it, you have hope for the future, and your wishes will come true.

Proverbs 24:13-14 NCV

The illiterate of the 21st century will not be those who cannot read and write, but those who cannot learn, unlearn, and relearn.

Alvin Toffler

*D*on't copy the behavior and customs of this world, but let God transform you into a new person by changing the way you think. Then you will learn to know God's will for you, which is good and pleasing and perfect.

Romans 12:2 NLT

*L*eadership is a combination of strategy and character. If you must be without one, be without the strategy.

H. Norman Schwarzkopf

Love and truth form a good leader; sound leadership
is founded on loving integrity.

Proverbs 20:28 THE MESSAGE

What lies behind us and what lies before us are tiny matters compared to what lies within us.

Ralph Waldo Emerson

*You're blessed when you're content with just who you are—
no more, no less. That's the moment you find yourselves
proud owners of everything that can't be bought.*

Matthew 5:5 THE MESSAGE

Do you know the difference between education and experience? Education is when you read the fine print; experience is what you get when you don't.

Pete Seeger

Those who refuse correction hate themselves, but those who accept correction gain understanding. Respect for the Lord will teach you wisdom. If you want to be honored, you must be humble.

Proverbs 15:32-33 NCV

*H*ope, like the gleaming taper's light,
Adorns and cheers our way;
And still, as darker grows the night,
Emits a brighter ray.

Oliver Goldsmith

*T*herefore I...do not cease to give thanks for you, making mention of you in my prayers: that the God of our Lord Jesus Christ, the Father of glory, may give to you the spirit of wisdom...; that you may know what is the hope of His calling.

EPHESIANS 1:15-18 NKJV

The true meaning of life is to plant trees under whose
shade you do not expect to sit.

Nelson Henderson

*I*t's not important who does the planting, or who does the watering. What's important is that God makes the seed grow. The one who plants and the one who waters work together with the same purpose. And both will be rewarded.

1 Corinthians 3:7-8 NLT

*N*o pessimist ever discovered the secrets of the stars, or sailed to an uncharted land, or opened a new heaven to the human spirit.

Helen Keller

pray that from His glorious, unlimited resources He will empower you with inner strength through His Spirit. Then Christ will make His home in your hearts as you trust in Him. Your roots will grow down into God's love and keep you strong.

Ephesians 3:16-17 NLT

We are made to persist. That's how we find out who we are.

Tobias Wolff

And so I tell you, keep on asking, and you will receive what you ask for. Keep on seeking, and you will find. Keep on knocking, and the door will be opened to you.

Luke 11:9 NLT

Learn as much as you can while you are young,
since life becomes too busy later.

Dana Stewart Scott

....

....

....

....

....

....

....

....

....

....

....

....

....

....

....

....

....

*Do not let anyone treat you as if you are unimportant because you
are young. Instead, be an example...with your words, your actions,
your love, your faith, and your pure life.*

1 Timothy 4:12 NCV

What we are is God's gift to us. What we become is our gift to God.

Eleanor Powell

For the Lord God is our sun and our shield. He gives us grace and glory. The Lord will withhold no good thing from those who do what is right.

Psalm 84:11 NLT

The victory of success is half won when one gains the habit of setting goals and achieving them. Even the most tedious chore will become endurable as you parade through each day convinced that every task, no matter how menial or boring, brings you closer to fulfilling your dreams.

Og Mandino

For our light and momentary troubles are achieving for us an eternal glory that far outweighs them all. So we fix our eyes not on what is seen, but on what is unseen. For what is seen is temporary, but what is unseen is eternal.

2 Corinthians 4:17-18 NIV

We learn more by looking for the answer to a question and not finding it than we do from learning the answer itself.

Lloyd Alexander

You will search again for the Lord your God. And if you search for
Him with all your heart and soul, you will find Him.

Deuteronomy 4:29 NLT

I hope your dreams take you to the corners of your smiles,
to the highest of your hopes, to the windows of your opportunities,
and to the most special places your heart has ever known.